# Advent & Christmas

# Worship Feast™

## Complete Worship Outlines for Advent and Christmas

**Abingdon Press**
**Nashville**

Complete Worship Outlines for Advent and Christmas

MANUFACTURED IN THE UNITED STATES OF AMERICA

08 09 10 11 12 13 14 15 17 18—10 9 8 7 6 5 4 3 2 1

COVER DESIGN: KEELY MOORE

# Contents

# Meet the Writers

**Jenny Youngman** has worked and worshiped with youth for ten years. She is the creator of the WORSHIP FEAST series for youth groups, and she is passionate about creative worship. Jenny leads workshops and worship gatherings for youth retreats and youth worker events. She lives with her family outside of Nashville, TN. To hear more of Jenny's music, visit *jennyyoungman.com*.

**Josh Tinley** is an editor for Abingdon Youth, a high school Sunday school teacher, a blogger, and an occasional freelance writer and workshop leader. Before attending Vanderbilt Divinity School, Josh spent six years in an independent rock band. He continues to write and perform music (though not nearly as often as he used to). Josh lives outside Nashville with his wife Ashlee, his children Meyer and Resha Kate, a soon-to-be third child, and too many cats.

# Worship Feast
# Advent &
# Christmas

# Worshiping Through Advent

The season of Advent begins the Christian year. In Advent we learn to wait, to expect God's movement in the world. The most familiar Advent tradition is the lighting of the Advent wreath. Even churches that do not strictly follow the liturgical calendar make a point to read Advent reflections and light Advent candles. It's a physical ritual that helps us anticipate the light of Christ coming into our world.

In the lives of teenagers, or any of us for that matter, it would be so easy to arrive at Christmas Day having shopped, partied, eaten, stressed about the perfect gifts, stressed about having enough money to buy the perfect gifts, and yet to have completely missed the hope that awaits us throughout the season of Advent. During the holiday season, just look at the news stories about shoppers lined up in the early morning hours and fighting one another to get inside the door. Most every year someone is assaulted while arguing over the year's "hottest" Christmas gift. Seems like we just don't have it in us to wait or to patiently take in the wonder of the season.

But at the very core of Advent is a patient expectation that God is about to do something. Every inch towards Christmas morning is filled with anticipation that God is going to burst onto the scene in a big way. God is coming to our world to save us, to know us, and to love us. And this is the truth we've been anxiously awaiting.

Sure, you may still procrastinate, waiting till the day before to complete all of your Christmas preparations. But this year I want to challenge you to savor the anticipation of Advent. Let your heart be giddy about what God is bringing to the world. Prepare room in your heart for the baby Jesus.

This year, during the Advent and Christmas season, take your youth group on a worship-filled journey from the wilderness to the manger. Be intentional about stopping amid the fast pace of the "city sidewalks." And may your Advent be filled with wonder, expectancy, patience, awe—and most of all—worship.

—Jenny Youngman

# How to Use Worship Feast Advent and Christmas

## A Guide to Services

This is a collection of worship services and ideas for the entire season of Advent and Christmas. You can do all of them or just a few, or even mix up the ideas to do your own thing. The themes of the services spring from the worship songs on the WORSHIP FEAST CD in the back of this book. Creativity and the invitation of the Holy Spirit are key to making these services come alive for your group.

We encourage you to offer several worship experiences for your youth this Advent. In this Advent and Christmas season, you will focus on worshiping God with all of your heart, soul, mind, and strength. Invite your students to prepare room in their hearts through these worship experiences and to allow God to fill their hearts with love for them.

## A Guide to the Starters

Included on page 41 are short "starters" for Sunday school, youth group, or other gatherings that bring your attention to the Advent season. The prayers are meant to supplement your group meeting times. Ask different students to lead them each week and let them be a time of centering. Light a candle as you say the prayer, and invite the living Christ to be your Lord.

## A Guide to Worship Feast Songs

In the back of this book is a CD that includes five original songs for worship during Advent and Christmas. You can make copies of the CD for your youth to listen to and learn the songs. The book also includes chords and lyrics for the songs beginning on page 42. Feel free to make copies of these for your student musicians.

Throughout the book, there are suggested songs, but feel free to add others or to add more group singing to the services.

Get to know these songs, and through them, let your hearts worship the newborn King. They were written especially for your group and for this special Advent season.

Services

# Baby Jesus, Come to Save Us

**Theme:** The need for salvation

**Scripture:** *"O that you would tear open the heavens and come down, so that the mountains would quake at your presence—as when fire kindles brushwood and the fire causes water to boil—to make your name known to your adversaries, so that the nations might tremble at your presence!" (Isaiah 64:1-2).*

**How the Youth Will Engage God:**
The first three worship services in WORSHIP FEAST ADVENT & CHRISTMAS are calls for the baby Jesus to "save us," to "know us," and to "love us." They are listed as separate services, but feel free to combine them for a longer worship experience.

Begin your Advent worship with a focus on the need for salvation. Think about the lives of your youth—all of the stress and hurts they may be experiencing. Read the following Scriptures that express the "God, save me" cry, the one to which we all can relate.

Youth will examine their deepest needs and ask God to meet them at that place.

**Supplies:** CD player, WORSHIP FEAST ADVENT & CHRISTMAS CD, *THE MESSAGE*, posterboard, paints, paintbrushes, tape or sticky tack

## —⚬— THE SERVICE —⚬—

**Sing Together:**
   ✳ *"Come, Thou Long-Expected Jesus"*
   ✳ *"O Come, O Come, Emmanuel"*

**Pray:**
Pray the following prayer or ask a volunteer
to lead the group in prayer:

*"Baby Jesus, we pray that you would come into our world
and save us from our sin and from the hurts that we
experience here on earth. We pray that we would know you
as our Savior, even as a baby in the manger. Come, baby
Jesus, and save us. Amen."*

**Worship Together:**
Play "Baby Jesus" from the WORSHIP FEAST ADVENT &
CHRISTMAS CD in the back of this book, or ask your
youth praise band to sing the song.

**Read the Scripture: Isaiah 64**
NOTE: Before you lead this service, enlist some of your
really great readers to rehearse this passage as a
readers theater-style reading. Assign verses and include
time for them to practice inflection and artistic delivery.
After the previous song, ask the students to stand up
wherever they are and to spontaneously begin the
reading. (*THE MESSAGE* has a great paraphrase of the
passage that would also be good to use for this style
reading.)

**Share the Message:**
Ahead of time think about what you want to say about why you personally need saving. You may or may not want to talk about specific situations in your life, but convey the gist of a deep need that helps you tangibly experience salvation. Or, you could tell about a time when you were "saved" from something during your teenage years. The point is to motivate the students' thinking about how they might feel or experience the salvation of God. **Isaiah 64:7b** says, "Because you've turned away from us, left us to stew in our sins" (*THE MESSAGE*). Imagine yourself being at that point—being in need of a Savior that desperately—and speak from your heart.

**Desperate Acrostic**
1. Provide each student a sheet of posterboard and access to some paints and paintbrushes.

2. On the left-hand side of the posterboard, youth should paint vertically the word *Desperate*. Then youth should create an acrostic poem describing their need for a Savior. Encourage students to be creative with the paints and lettering. Here is an example:

**D** eep
**E** motions
**S** in
**P** rayers
**E** nough
**R** age
**A** nyone
**T** here?
**E** verywhere.

**3.** Play the CD in the back of this book as background music while students create their acrostic poems. When they are finished, provide tape or sticky tack so that youth may display their posters on the walls as symbols for your worship space.

### Closing:
When everyone's poster has been displayed, gather students together and lead in saying the closing litany.

ONE:   O God, we are tired.
ALL:   *O that you would tear open the heavens and come down.*
ONE:   O God, we are sinners.
ALL:   *O that you would tear open the heavens and come down.*
ONE:   O God, we need you to save us.
ALL:   *O that you would tear open the heavens and come down.*
ONE:   O God, do not leave us to stew in our sin.
ALL:   *O that you would tear open the heavens and come down.*
ONE:   Come, baby Jesus.
ALL:   *O that you would tear open the heavens and come down.*

# Baby Jesus, Come to Know Us

**Theme:** The need to be known

**Scripture:** *"This is the kind of life you've been invited into, the kind of life Christ lived. He suffered everything that came his way so you would know that it could be done, and also know how to do it, step-by-step"* (1 Peter 2:21, THE MESSAGE).

**How the Youth Will Engage God:**
Humans have a need to be known—to have friends who know us well. Jesus came to save us, but he also came to know us. The fact that Jesus knows us helps us to depend on him and trust him as a friend. We can trust his salvation because he knows everything we experience. We can trust his strength because he has been tried far beyond what we face in our lives.

Youth will meet God in the act of putting back together the broken pieces of their lives.

**Supplies:** CD player, WORSHIP FEAST ADVENT & CHRISTMAS CD, *THE MESSAGE*, blank tiles or bricks, a variety of smooth-edged, broken glass pieces, beads, buttons, stones and marbles, texture paint or colored grout, glaze

## —ᵐᵛ— THE SERVICE —ᵐᵛ—

**Sing Together:**
✳ "Baby Jesus" (from the CD in the
back of this book)

**Read the Scripture:**
Enlist one of your good readers to read
aloud **1 Peter 2:21** from *THE MESSAGE*.

**Pray:**
Pray this prayer or one of your own:

*"Baby Jesus, we are so grateful that you came to live
among us. Thank you for taking on our lives so that you
would know our pain, struggles, and fears. Take our
brokenness and put us back together. Create something
beautiful in us. Amen."*

**Know Us Mosaic**
**1.** Give each student a blank tile or brick. Lay out a
variety of smooth-edged, broken glass pieces, beads,
buttons, stones, and marbles. Allow students to
choose their pieces to create a mosaic.

**2.** Instruct youth to spread the texture paint or easy-
spread, colored grout over the surface of the blank
tiles or bricks, then press the glass pieces into the
grout. When the grout is dry (and if you have time),
students may add a coat of glaze to their mosaics.

**3.** As youth create their mosaics, encourage them to meditate on the truth that Jesus knows us and restores us out of brokenness. Suggest they choose stones that represent for them the broken areas of their lives.

**4.** Play the CD in the back of this book as background music while the students work.

**Meditate:**
**1.** When the mosaics are completed, ask the youth to place them on and around an altar table. (Be careful, because the tiles may still be wet.)

**2.** Invite students to become comfortable and clear their minds. Encourage them to create space in their hearts to meet Christ. Once everyone is settled, begin the following guided meditation.

"Does anybody really know me? know what I go through? (*pause*) I walk the halls of my school, and I smile and wave at people passing by—hoping that no one looks too closely into my eyes. (*pause*) If they looked harder they'd see the hurts that I cover up. They'd see the fears that I pretend I don't have. They'd see that I feel tossed around here, like I can't get or keep my feet on the ground. (*pause*)

And then I hear it—a word of hope: "This is the kind of life you've been invited into, the kind of life Christ lived. He suffered everything that came his way so [you] would know that it could be done, and also how to do it, step-by-step" (**1 Peter 2:21**, *THE MESSAGE*). (*pause*)

Jesus knows this road I walk. Jesus has felt my tears. Jesus showed me that I can do this. I can lift my head and experience joy. Jesus makes broken things beautiful. (*pause*)

Jesus makes broken things beautiful. (*pause*)

Jesus makes broken things beautiful.

**Closing:**
Pause briefly, then say the following prayer.

*"Loving God, we are so grateful that you sent your Son to walk among us and know what we go through in our lives. This Advent we pray that you would lead us to the manger and that we would experience the beautiful life that comes to us in Jesus Christ. As the Christmas flurries surround us, help us to be still and wait with anticipation for the Savior of the world to come for us. Baby Jesus, come to know us. Amen."*

# Baby Jesus, Come to Love Us

**Theme:** The truth that Jesus came to love us

**Scripture:** *"For God so loved the world that he gave his only Son, so that everyone who believes in him may not perish but may have eternal life"* (John 3:16).

**How the Youth Will Engage God:**
**John 3:16** is probably the most memorized verse in the entire Bible. Many of us know the verse backwards and forwards—and that is great! But sometimes, when we know something so well, we skim over it and miss the true meaning. God *so* loved the world. In other words, God loved the world so much that God stooped from heaven to become like us—to save us, to know us, and most of all to love us.

The love of God is what Advent and Christmas are all about—God loving us so much that God chose to come into our world. Help your youth experience this love by meditating on each word of **John 3:16**. Instead of skimming the verse quickly, savor every word with gratitude and joy.

**Supplies:** CD player, Christmas songs

# —ᴡᴠ— THE SERVICE —ᴠᴡ—

**Read the Scripture:**
Begin the service by spontaneously reciting **John 3:16**. Repeat the verse a few times and then invite the youth to join you. Continue saying the verse as a chant, building louder and then tapering off after a minute or so.

**Sing Together:**
Choose several favorite Christmas songs to sing together. Include the following:
* ✳ "Here I Am to Worship"
* ✳ "Baby Jesus" (from the CD in the back of this book)

**Meditate:**
**1.** Invite the youth to spread out across the room, but within hearing distance, and find places where they can relax and sit comfortably.

**2.** Explain that you will lead them in *lectio divina* or "spiritual reading." Say: I will read **John 3:16** three times, and each time you will listen differently as I guide you." Wait in a moment of silence while everyone prepares.

**3.** Say: "As I read our Scripture, allow your heart to soak in the words. Open your heart to experience God's love." Read aloud **John 3:16**, then pause for 2 to 3 minutes.

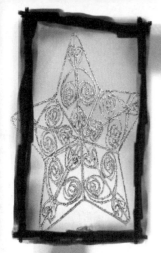

**4.** Say: "As I read the verse again, pay attention to a word or phrase that jumps out at you. Repeat the word or phrase in your mind and imagine what God might be saying to you." Read **John 3:16** and then pause for 3 to 4 minutes.

**5.** Say: "I will read the passage one more time. This time, as you hear the words, imagine that God's love is pouring over you like a rain shower. Soak in the love of God, deep in your heart and soul. Know the love of God as you hear these words." Read **John 3:16** once more and pause for 4 to 5 minutes of silence. (*Optional:* If you have a rain stick, move it back and forth as you read the Scripture this time.)

**6.** Close the meditation by praying that God would fill each student's heart with the knowledge of God's love.

**7.** Gather youth together and allow any who wish to talk about their meditation experiences. Ask any who wish to tell the words that grabbed their attention or to talk about any God-moments they experienced.

**Closing:**
Choose a song to sing together and then say this benediction.

*"May you know the love of God deep in your heart and soul, and may you experience Christmas in a new way this year. Come, baby Jesus, Come! Amen."*

# The Word

**Theme:** Christ as the Word, or Logos, of God

**Scripture:** *"In the beginning was the Word, and the Word was with God, and the Word was God"* (John 1:1).

**How the Youth Will Engage God:**
Youth will consider how a word is more than just a series of letters; it is a series of letters that conveys sounds and meanings. When you read the word *banana*, you can hear the sounds of the consonants and vowels and picture a long, yellow fruit. In this service, youth will gain a better understanding of Jesus as the Word of God. Just as a word is more than a series of letters, Jesus was more than just a human being. His life and ministry conveyed to the world who God is and God's will for creation.

**Supplies:** Sheets of paper or PowerPoint® slides prepared with examples of common nouns, blank sheets of drawing paper, markers and/or colored pencils

**Instructions:**
Beforehand prepare four or five sheets of paper or PowerPoint® slides, writing (or typing) in large letters a common noun on each sheet of paper or slide. Select words representing items that would be easy to draw (such as *tree, car, church,* or *fish*).

## —ᴧᴧ— THE SERVICE —ᴧᴧ—

**1.** Display your prepared word sheets in your worship space or run your prepared PowerPoint® slides in a loop.

**2.** Give each participant some drawing paper and markers and/or colored pencils. Ask the participants to spend a few minutes drawing the images that come to mind when they read the words you've presented. During this time, play quiet, repetitive, background music (such as the song "The Word" from the CD in the back of this book).

**Read the Scripture:**
**1.** After a few minutes read aloud **John 1:1-18** or ask several youth to help you read the verses. Then say: "Look at the images you've drawn. I gave you a word, a series of letters; you were able to look at that word and see something more: You saw an image of a car or a tree or a fish." (Substitute your words accordingly.)

**2.** Explain that words give us order and structure; they give us names for objects, actions, and concepts; and words allow us to discuss these objects, actions, and concepts with other people.

**Share the Message:**
**1.** Say: "Jesus is the Word of God. John's Gospel tells us that Christ gives order and structure to God's creation. Jesus came into our world as an infant and lived among us. When we read the stories of Jesus' birth, life, and ministry, we gain a sense of who God is and of God's will for creation. Just as a word—a series of letters—conveys an image of an object or idea, Jesus' earthly life conveys an image of God and of God's kingdom."

**2.** Explain that "Word" in **John 1:1-18** is a translation of the Greek word *logos*. *Logos* does not simply refer to a word that is written or spoken. In ancient Greek thought, *logos* referred to the divine principle or pattern that gave order to the entire universe and connects us with God. By referring to Jesus as the Logos, John is saying that Christ gave structure to the world and gave us a path to God.

**Lead a Litany:**
Invite the youth to spend a moment in silence, then lead youth in saying the litany on the next page.

**Sing Together:**
 ✳ "The Word" (from the CD in the back of this book)

**Closing:**
As a benediction, read aloud **John 1:18**. Say a closing prayer, thanking God for sending Jesus to give us a fuller sense of who God is and what God wills for creation.

# Because Jesus Was . . .
## Litany

**LEADER:** Because Jesus was born in a stable . . .

**PEOPLE:** We know that God is humble.

**LEADER:** Because Jesus was a healer . . .

**PEOPLE:** We know that God heals.

**LEADER:** Because Jesus taught about justice . . .

**PEOPLE:** We know that God is just.

**LEADER:** Because Jesus welcomed all people . . .

**PEOPLE:** We know that God does not play favorites.

**LEADER:** Because Jesus wept . . .

**PEOPLE:** We know that God suffers with us.

**LEADER:** Because Jesus forgave those who had wronged him . . .

**PEOPLE:** We know that God is forgiving.

**LEADER:** Because Jesus died . . .

**PEOPLE:** We know that God's love for us knows no limits.

**LEADER:** Because Jesus rose from the grave . . .

**PEOPLE:** We know that God is greater than death.

# Delicious Redemption

**Theme:** God's ongoing redemption of the world

**Scripture:** *"The vessel [the potter] was making of clay was spoiled in the potter's hand, and he reworked it into another vessel, as seemed good to him. Then the word of the LORD came to [Jeremiah]: 'Can I not do with you, O house of Israel, just as this potter has done?'"* (Jeremiah 18:4-6a).

**How the Youth Will Engage God:**
Youth will get a taste (literally) of how God in Christ redeems our broken world.

**Supplies:** One candy cane for each youth, two pounds of white chocolate, a double boiler, a cookie sheet covered in waxed paper, a mallet

**Optional:** peppermint flavoring, a copy of *Good God Theater Act 1: Old Testament DVD* (see page 31)

**Instructions:**
Shortly before your worship experience, melt two pounds of white chocolate in a double boiler. If you wish, add a little peppermint flavoring to the melted chocolate. Take the melted chocolate to your worship space. (If possible, transfer it to a Crock-Pot® so that it will stay soft during your worship experience.)

# —m— THE SERVICE —m—

1. Give each participant a candy cane. (If you have few participants, hand out large candy canes; if you have several people, hand out small candy canes.)

2. Say: "The prophet Jeremiah knew all about brokenness. During his career, the Kingdom of Judah strayed from God and was conquered by the Babylonians. The Babylonians demolished the Temple and forced many of Judah's people into exile. God instructed Jeremiah to illustrate Judah's brokenness in several ways."

**Read the Scripture:**
1. Ask a volunteer to read aloud **Jeremiah 13:1-11**, preferably from *THE MESSAGE*. (God tells Jeremiah to ruin a pair of linen shorts.)

2. Ask a second volunteer to read aloud **Jeremiah 19:1-6, 10-11**. (God tells Jeremiah to break an earthenware jug.)

**Share the Message:**
1. Say: "Think of one way that you are broken, hurting, or struggling. As you think about this brokenness, break your candy cane into pieces." If the youth have small candy canes that are packaged in plastic pouches, they should leave the canes in the pouches as they break or crush them. If the youth have large, shrink-wrapped candy canes, direct them to remove the wrapping and simply snap the candy canes in two.

**2.** Gather the broken candy-cane pieces in a large, plastic zipper-bag. Hand the bag and a mallet to a volunteer. Ask youth to call out examples of brokenness, pain, sin, and death in our world. (*Examples might include war, disease, poverty, fear, racism, and so on.*) As each example is named, tell the volunteer to hit the bag of candy with the mallet, breaking the canes into even smaller peppermint pieces.

**3.** Say, "Fortunately God had another metaphor in store for Jeremiah—one that said that brokenness would not be the end of the story." Ask another volunteer to read aloud **Jeremiah 18:1-6** (the potter and the clay). Say, "Just as the potter was able to redeem the pottery that had fallen apart in his hands, God can redeem a creation that has fallen into sin and death."

**Sing Together:**
Pour the broken, peppermint-candy pieces into the melted chocolate you prepared earlier. As you stir the candy into the chocolate, sing together the song "Redemption" (from the CD in the back of this book).

**Closing:**
**1.** Say, "God's plan for redemption involved sending God's only Son into the world to heal us, to teach us, and to deliver us from sin, death, and brokenness."

**2.** Pour the chocolate-and-candy mixture onto the layered cookie sheet. Say: "Just as the melted chocolate transformed our broken candy canes into something new and delicious, and just as the potter was able to make something new with the pottery that fell apart in his hands, Christ heals our brokenness and makes each one of us into a new creation."

**3.** Ask a volunteer to read aloud **Jeremiah 31:31-34** (a new covenant) as a benediction, then say a closing prayer thanking God for redemption.

**4.** Place the cookie sheet in the refrigerator. After 45 minutes, you and your youth will taste sweet redemption as you enjoy delicious peppermint bark.

**Option:**
Show the "Advent" segment from *Good God Theater Act 1: Old Testament* (DVD, Abingdon Youth 2008; ISBN-13: 978068746701). In this segment, God reveals to Gabriel the plan to redeem creation by sending God's Son to earth as a child born to a virgin.

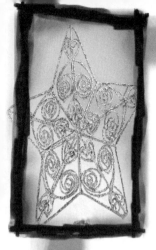

# He Shall Be Called Jesus

**Theme: The narrative of Jesus' birth**

**Scripture:** *"And now, you will conceive in your womb and bear a son, and you will name him Jesus. He will be great, and will be called the Son of the Most High, and the Lord God will give to him the throne of his ancestor David. He will reign over the house of Jacob forever, and of his kingdom there will be no end"* (Luke 1:31-33).

**How the Youth Will Engage God:**
This worship serivce is a journey through the entire narrative of Jesus' birth. Beginning with John the Baptist, youth will "travel" through the story, arriving with the shepherds to worship the newborn King. This service offers a series of prayer stations through which youth will travel.

**Supplies:** Bibles, CD player and CDs for background music, candles and matches for use in all five prayer stations, prayer station supplies(see pages 33-35)

**Instructions:** Make copies of the Prayer Station Guides on pages 36–40. Provide copies of the Guides at each station.

## —⚡— THE SERVICE —⚡—

**Introduction to the Journey:**
Set the stage for the worship experience by telling the youth that they are about to travel through the story of Jesus' birth. Explain that each stop is a prayer station offering them the opportunity to connect to the story, reflect, and pray before moving on. Play some background music as they travel through the stations.

### Prayer Station 1: John the Baptist
**1.** Cover a small table using green fabric. Lay out some twigs, a piece of leather, a megaphone, and a bowl of honey. Place a candle and matches in the center of the items.

**2.** Also set out several Bibles opened to **Matthew 3:1-12**. Youth should read the Scripture passage once or twice, then pray for the prophetic voice that John had to make the way plain for Christ. When they're ready, students should speak into the megaphone, saying "Prepare the way of the Lord!" and move on to the next station.

### Prayer Station 2: Joseph the Carpenter
**1.** Lay a piece of wood, a hammer, and some nails on a table along with candles and matches.

**2.** Provide several Bibles opened to **Matthew 1:18-25**. Youth should read through the Scripture passage a few times, then pray for courage to trust God's leading. Finally, students will hammer nails into the piece of wood.

### Prayer Station 3: Mary the Young Girl

**1.** Collect and display on a table some figurines of Mary from a variety of nativity sets, paper, pens or pencils, and several candles and matches.

**2.** Provide Bibles opened to **Luke 1:26-56**. Students should read through the Scripture passage a few times. After they have prayed through the Scripture, encourage them to memorize verse 38 by copying the verse several times on paper.

### Prayer Station 4: Jesus the Messiah

**1.** Set out diapers, bottles, and baby blankets on a table. Next to these items, set up a small Christmas tree. Arrange several Bibles opened to **Luke 2:1-7**. Youth should read through the Scripture passage a few times.

**2.** Provide a variety of craft supplies and construction paper for youth to make Chrismons. Once the Chrismons are complete, youth may hang them on the tree. (Instructions for making Chrismons are on the Prayer Station Guide handout on page 39.)

### Prayer Station 5: The Shepherds and the Angels

**1.** Display several stuffed-animal sheep and some children's dress-up angel costumes. Provide several Bibles opened to **Luke 2:8-20**.

**2.** Provide posterboard and markers or paints for youth to design posters declaring, "Glory to God." When they're finished with their posters, suggest youth hang them on the walls.

**Closing:**

**1.** When youth have traveled through all of the prayer stations, gather as a large group. Talk through the narrative of Jesus' birth (*John the Baptist preparing the way, Joseph's change of heart, Mary's "yes," Jesus' birth, the angel appearing to the shepherds, and the shepherds worshiping Jesus*).

**2.** Sing together "Infant Holy" (from the CD in the back of this book). Close by saying the following prayer or one of your own.

*"God, we are so grateful for your marvelous plan to bring about salvation for the children that you so deeply love. Help us to find ourselves in this story and to learn to say "yes" like Mary and to worship like the shepherds. You are wonderful, Lord. Come into our world and receive our worship. Amen."*

# Prayer Station Guide

## JOHN THE BAPTIST

John the Baptist was somewhat of an odd bird. He did not live the conventional life of other villagers and townspeople. He was a roamer. The Bible says he ate locusts and wild honey and wore camel-hair clothes and leather belts. But John's entire mission in life was to wake up people to the coming of Jesus Christ. He went around yelling at people to repent and to prepare for Jesus' coming.

1. **Prayerfully read Matthew 3:1-12 a few times. Pray for the prophetic voice that John had to make the way plain for Christ.**

2. **When you're ready, and before moving on to the next station, pick up the megaphone and shout into it, "Prepare the way of the Lord!"**

# Prayer Station Guide

## JOSEPH THE CARPENTER

Joseph was going about his life doing the carpenter thing and getting ready to live the married life. Then, all of a sudden, Mary announces that she is having a baby. Well, of course, he'd think she was a little nuts with the whole "angel appearing" story. He decides to divorce her quietly and sweep the whole thing under the rug. But God had other plans. Joseph gets his own "angel appearing" story and becomes a part of the story of God's redemption.

1. Prayerfully read Joseph's story in Matthew 1:18-25 a few times. Pray for courage to trust God's leading.

2. When you're ready to move on, hammer a nail into the piece of wood, while imagining the faithful courage of this carpenter-turned-daddy-to-be.

# Prayer Station Guide

## MARY THE YOUNG GIRL

Mary is revered for her faithfulness, her worship, and her simple trust in God's leading. This was no small thing that God asked of her. She risked her pride, her reputation, her marriage, even her life. Her "yes" brought the Messiah into the world.

1. Prayerfully read Luke 1:26-56 a few times. Imagine if you were Mary. Would you be so quick to say "yes"? Would you need a few days to decide? Pray for the courage to boldly say "yes," like Mary, when God calls you.

2. Practice saying "yes" to God by memorizing Mary's words in verse 38. Mary said, "Here am I, the servant of the Lord; let it be with me according to your word." As a memorization tool, use the paper and pencils to copy this verse several times. When you think you have memorized the verse, move on to the next prayer station.

# Prayer Station Guide

## JESUS THE MESSIAH

The Savior of the world came to us as a tiny baby born in a barn. He didn't arrive to the sound of trumpet blasts and national celebration. He came quietly and humbly to an unlikely young couple.

1. Prayerfully read Luke 2:1-7 a few times, then pray worshipfully to the newborn King.

2. Use the craft supplies to create a Chrismon. The word *Chrismon* is an abbreviation for the term *Christ Monogram*. A Chrismon can be one of a variety of Christian symbols that represent the person, life, or story of Jesus Christ. Most properly, a Chrismon incorporates the letters of Jesus' name; an example is the Chi-Rho symbol, which consists of the Greek letters *Chi* (X) and *Rho* (P) superimposed together. Once your Chrismon is complete, hang it on the tree and move to the next prayer station.

# Prayer Station Guide

## THE SHEPHERD AND THE ANGELS

Who doesn't remember the children's Christmas plays in which adorable little girls are dressed up in white gowns, ballet slippers, and shiny, gold halos? And the cute little guys wearing burlap cloaks and carrying shepherds' crooks while walking up the aisle? That might be how we reinact the story, but imagine being out in the middle of a field in the middle of the night and suddenly seeing angels appear. Imagine the wonder these guys must have experienced—wonder that was followed by belief and then worship of the baby Christ Child.

1. Prayerfully read Luke 2:8-20 a few times. Pray for wonder and awe at the amazing ways God speaks to us. Pray for a heart to worship as the shepherds did.

2. Now use the supplies to create a poster declaring "Glory to God" and hang it on the wall.

# Starters

Use these Starters at the beginning of Bible studies, meetings, or other gatherings.

## 1 Light the First Advent Candle.

*Read* aloud **Isaiah 60:1-3**. *Invite* someone to light the candle. *Say*: "This candle reminds us that Christ is our hope. We hope. We believe. We trust in God's salvation. May the light of God light our path to the manger."

## 2 Light the Second Advent Candle.

*Ask* a volunteer to read aloud **Mark 1:4**. *Invite* someone to light the candles. *Say*: "We light this candle to remind us that Jesus shows us the way to God. We will follow the way."

## 3 Light the Third Advent Candle.

*Ask* a volunteer to read aloud **Isaiah 35:10**. *Invite* someone to light the candles. *Say*: "We light this candle to remind us that Christ is our joy. We walk the way of Jesus filled with joy."

## 4 Light the Fourth Advent Candle.

*Ask* a volunteer to read aloud **Isaiah 9:6-7**. *Invite* someone to light the candles. *Say*: "We light this candle to remind us that Jesus is the Prince of Peace."

## 5 Light the Christmas Candle.

*Ask* a volunteer to read aloud **Isaiah 9:2-7**. *Invite* someone to light the candles. *Say*: "We light this candle to celebrate the light of Jesus Christ coming into our world."

# Redemption

*Chorus (sung throughout)*

Gm    F ┊ Eb    Dm ┊ Gm   F ┊ Eb    Dm    ┊ Gm    F   Eb   Dm ┊ Gm   F ┊ Eb      Dm
Lord, redeem our broken world;          Lord, redeem our broken world.

*Verse 1*

┊ Gm      F ┊ Eb        Dm ┊ Gm     F ┊ Eb       Dm ┊
Deliver us from fear and sadness, hopelessness and pain;

Gm         F ┊ Eb    Dm ┊ Gm      F ┊ Eb       Dm ┊
Save us from our apathy, our brokenness, our shame.

*Repeat Chorus*

*Verse 2*

Gm      F ┊ Eb     Dm ┊ Gm      F ┊ Eb      Dm ┊
Rescue us from pride and anger, selfishness and greed;

Gm      F ┊ Eb    Dm ┊ Gm      F ┊ Eb      Dm ┊
Give us hope and give us life, restore us, set us free.

*Repeat Chorus*

*Verse 3*

Gm     F ┊ Eb     Dm ┊ Gm     F ┊ Eb      Dm
Send us your anointed one to heal and make us whole,

┊ Gm      F ┊ Eb      Dm ┊ Gm    F ┊ Eb      Dm       ┊
To break the bonds of sin and death, to lift our weary souls.

Words and music by Josh Tinley
© 2008 Josh Tinley

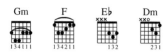

Gm       F       Eb      Dm
134111   134211   132    231

# Baby Jesus

*Verse 1*

G C D C G C D C

 Baby Jesus, come to save us from our sin and from ourselves.

G C D C G C D C

 We are poor and we are tired, we are lost here in this world.

*Verse 2*

G C D C G C D C

 Baby Jesus, come to know us, feel our tears and live our pain.

G C D C G C D C

 We've been broken, we've been battered, we felt hopeless and afraid.

*Refrain*

Em D C D Em D C D

 Precious baby, holy child. Oh, how desperately we need you.

Em D C D Em D C D

 Precious baby, holy child. Oh, how desperately we need you.

*Verse 3*

G C D C G C D C

 Baby Jesus, come to love us, deep within our hearts and souls;

G C D C G C D C

 Give us knowledge of your father's love for us that makes us whole.

*Repeat Chorus*

Words and music by Jenny Youngman
© 2008 Jenny Youngman

G  C  D  Em

# The Word

*Verse 1*

D      Em      D   Em      D   Em   D   Em

In the beginning was the Word  (the Word was God).

  D      Em      D   Em      D   Em   D   Em

The Word was the source of everything  (the Word was God).

  D      Em   D   Em   D      Em      D      Em

The Word brought life into being, the life was the light of all people.

  D      Em   D      Em      D   Em   D      Em

The darkness did not overcome it   (the Word was God).

*Verse 2*

D      Em      D   Em      D   Em   D      Em

There was a man sent from God  (his name was John);

  D      Em      D   Em      D   Em   D      Em

He came as a witness to the light   (his name was John).

  D      Em      D   Em      D      Em      D      Em

He came so that all might believe that the light which enlightens is coming,

  D   Em      D   Em      D   Em   D      Em

But he himself was not the light  (his name was John).

Words and music by Josh Tinley
© 2008 Josh Tinley

*Verse 3*

| D | Em | D | Em | D | Em | D | Em |

The Word came to live as one of us   (the Son of God);

D | Em | D | Em | D | Em | D | Em

He became flesh like one of us   (the Son of God).

| D | Em | D | Em | D | Em | D | Em

Now we have seen his glory,    the glory of a father's only son.

D | Em | D | Em | D | Em | D | Em

Full of grace and truth   (the Son of God).

# He Shall Be Called Jesus

Bb | C | Bb | C

He shall be called Jesus.         He will be great, the Son of the Most Hig

| Bb | C | Bb | C

And he will reign in a kingdom without end,    and he shall be called Jesus.

Words and music by Jenny Youngman
© 2008 Jenny Youngman

# Infant Holy, Infant Lowly

*Verse 1*

G    Bm      C      D     G

    Infant holy, infant lowly, for his bed a cattle stall;

   Bm      C        D      G

oxen lowing, little knowing, Christ the babe is Lord of all.

   Bm    C    D    G     Bm    C     D

Christ the babe is Lord of all.

*Verse 2*

G     Bm       C       D        G

   Swift are winging angels singing, noels ringing, tidings bringing;

   Bm    C    D    G    Bm    C    D     G

Christ the babe is Lord of all.   Christ the babe is Lord of all.

*Verse 3*

Em                   Bm                C

   Flocks were sleeping, shepherds keeping vigil till the morning new

        D          Em

saw the glory, heard the story, tidings of a gospel true.

     Bm                C

Thus rejoicing, free from sorrow, praises voicing, greet the morrow;

   D    C    D   G

Christ the babe was born for you.

Words Polish carol; trans. by Edith M. G. Reed. Music Polish carol; arr. by Josh Tinley.
Arr. © 2008 Abingdon Press

G      Em      Bm      C      D

# More Worship Feast Resources

**1. Worship Feast: Complete Worship Outlines for Lent and Easter.** An exciting alternative to other Lent and Easter worship fare, including seven original worship songs recorded on a CD, along with printed lyrics and chords.

**2. Worship Feast Charles Wesley: 12 Worship Services Based on Wesley's Hymns.** Partners with the CD, *Love Divine*, to offer reflections and worship meditations on some great Wesley hymns. Reflections written by contemporary Christian artists.

**3. Worship Feast Prayer Stations.** A collection of video instructions for creating prayer stations and different ways to use them.

**4. Worship Feast: 8 Easy-to-Learn Dances for Worship** (DVD). Features step-by-step instructional choreography for liturgical dance for any skill level, including hymns, worship songs, and contemporary Christan music.

**5. Worship Feast: 20 Complete Services in the Spirit of Taizé.** Offers meditations, song suggestions, prayers, and silence. Includes a split-track, instrumental music CD.

*Note:* See the complete line of WORSHIP FEAST resources at *Abingdonyouth.com*

## WORSHIP FEAST ADVENT & CHRISTMAS SONGS

### THE PLAYERS

**Josh Tinley:** Vocals, Piano, Keys, Bass Guitar, Tamborine
**Jenny Youngman:** Vocals, Piano, Keys
**David Henry:** Background Vocals, Cello, Guitar
**Tommy Perkinson:** Drums